The BIBLE
Graphically Presented

"Study to shew thyself approved unto God, a workman that needeth not to be ashamed, rightly dividing the word of truth."

2 Timothy 2:15

Copyright © 2016 Randy White
Cover and Illustration: Leonardo Costa

All Scripture quotations, unless otherwise indicated, are taken from the King James Version.

All rights reserved. This book or any portion thereof may not be reproduced or used in any manner whatsoever without the express written permission of the publisher except for the use of brief quotations in a book review.

Printed in the United States of America

First Edition, First Printing, 2016

ISBN: 978-1-945774-02-7

Dispensational Publishing House, Inc.
220 Paseo del Pueblo Norte
Taos, NM 87571

www.dispensationalpublishing.com

Ordering Information:
Quantity sales. Special discounts are available on quantity purchases by churches, associations, and others. For details, contact the publisher at the address above.

Orders by U.S. trade bookstores and wholesalers. Please contact the publisher: Tel: (855) 437-9448

1 2 3 4 5 6 7 8 9 10

Contents

The Old Testament

The Hebrew Scriptures: A Historic Sweep 6

The Pre-National History of the Hebrew Nation 8

The National History of the Hebrew Nation 10

The Cycle of Sin in the Book of Judges 12

The Divided Kingdom and Beyond 14

The Divided Kingdom 16

Captivity and Return 18

Daniel's Vision of World History 20

The Chronological Old Testament 22

Between the Testaments 24

The New Testament

The Presentation of the King and His Kingdom 28

Has The Kingdom Arrived? 30

Prerequisites to the Kingdom of God 32

The Fall of Israel and the Rise of the Church (Acts) 34
The Chronological New Testament 36

The Book of Revelation 39

Comparison of Revelation Seals with Matthew 24 40
The Churches of Revelation | Historic View 42
The Churches of Revelation | Dynamic and Prophetic Views 44
The Churches of Revelation | Futurist View 46
An Alternate Chronology of the Book of Revelation 48

Theology

General 53

From Eternity to Eternity 54
Promise of a Coming One 56
Promise of a Returning One 58
Biblical Covenants 60
The Origin of Evil 62
The Work of Satan 64
Postmillennialism 66
Amillennialism 68

    Historic Premillennialism 70

    Dispensational Premillennialism 72

    Finding the Dispensations in the Bible 74

From the Old Testament 77

    The Chronological Suspension Bridge 78

    The Tablets of Genesis 80

From the New Testament 83

    Paul and The 12 Apostles 84

    The Prophetic Plan Revealed 86

    The Mystery Revealed 88

    Christ in the Scriptures 90

    Freedom In Christ 92

Chronological Timelines of the Old Testament 95

    Introduction to the Timelines 96

    Adam to Noah 97

    Noah to Abraham 98

    Abraham to Exodus 99

    Exodus to Monarchy 100

    Divided Kingdom 101

From the Author

Over the years of teaching, I have found that placing valuable information into chart form has helped me grasp the complete picture of the material. Doing so has also provided a long-lasting reference for the ones I teach. What you have in this book is the compilation of many of the charts I've used over the past few years. The origins of many of these charts was a college Bible study I led in our home. The materials of this study were used in the first of what became a popular "Six Hour Bible Study" series in which I would take participants through a major Bible theme from 6:00 PM to Midnight. Other charts were added from materials I prepared in teaching verse-by-verse through various segments of the Bible.

It is my prayer that you will find these charts to be helpful as you build your theology from the Word of God. As with any Biblical reference work or commentary, you should question the assumptions. The charts in this book are written with my own theological bias, just like any theological work ever printed. I pray that my bias is grounded in Scripture, but the Scripture stands as the only source of our authority for faith and practice. If you find any of these graphics to be Biblically incorrect, go with the 66 books of the Bible and not the 43 charts in this book.

Many of you will use this book as a personal Bible study aid. I hope you'll write in the note section so that you'll record insights that you can use to help yourself and others in days to come. Others of you will use this book in a classroom or seminar setting, and I pray that the insights gained from interactive discussion will be recorded in the notes section to make this book of even more value into the future.

I am grateful to the churches I've served. These churches received this information firsthand, and have seen my own mind and theology move over the years to what I hope is a solidly grounded Biblical position. I'm grateful that these churches have allowed me to study, learn, grow and change. What a wonderful blessing it is when a church encourages its pastor to learn!

This work could not have been accomplished in beauty without the very capable work of Leonardo Costa of Brazil. I met Leonardo on social media and initiated a conversation with him on a theological matter. Over time, I realized that he and I are both passionate about the same dispensational theology. As opportunity arose, I began to use him to help in graphic design, an area in which he is self-trained but greatly skilled. What a joy it is now to have him as a fellow-servant, taking what I do and making it beautiful to look at. It is rare to have a graphic designer who already knows dispensational theology and therefore doesn't need an interpretation of the material. He is a blessing beyond compare.

My prayer is that as you study to shew thyself approved that you will rightly divide the word of truth in a way that strengthens your faith, encourages your walk with the Lord, and is then used as you train others to understand the Bible.

Until He Comes—

Randy White,
Taos, NM

The Old Testament

The BIBLE
Graphically Presented

THE HEBREW SCRIPTURES
The Historic Sweep

PRE-NATIONAL HISTORY		NATIONAL HISTORY			
PRE-JEWISH	JEWISH	CONQUEST	JUDGES	MONARCHY	DIVIDED KINGDOM AND BEYOND
Genesis 1-11, Job	Genesis 12-Deuteronomy	Joshua	Judges Ruth 1 Samuel 1-7	1 Samuel 8-24 2 Samuel 1 Kings 1-11 1 Chronicles 2 Chronicles 1-11	1 Kings 12-22 2 Kings 2 Chronicles 10-36 Ezra, Nehemiah Esther

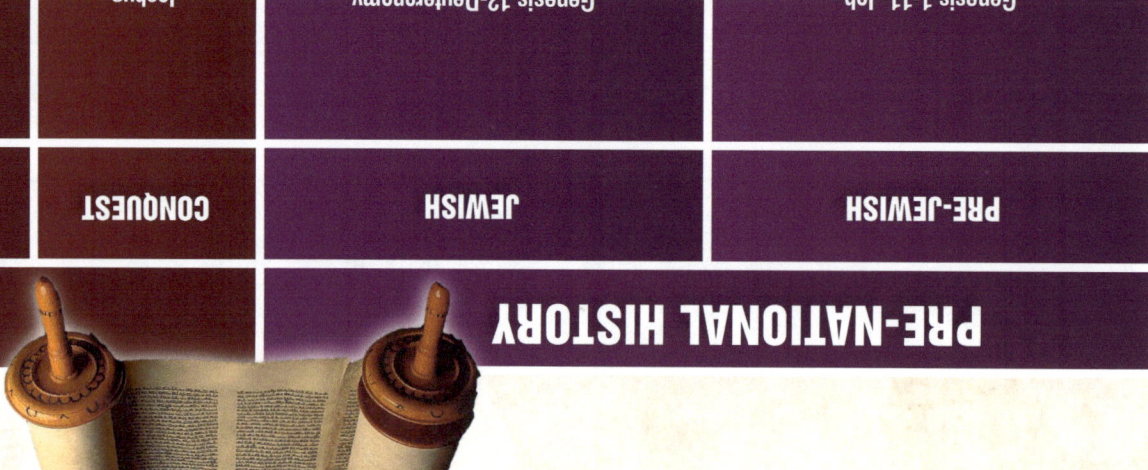

Description

The Hebrew Scriptures are often called the "Old Testament," but this is the language of Covenant Theology and was started with the Catholic scholar Jerome in the 4th Century. They are better called "Hebrew Scriptures," simply as a designation of the language in which they were written.

The historical section of the Hebrew Scriptures can be nicely divided into two segments: pre-national and national history, with the nation of Israel being the core people around which these books are written. Each of these segments further divides into historical segments. Knowing where a passage lies in this chart will help you understand the historical setting of the passage.

Notes

_____

_____

_____

_____

_____

_____

THE PRE-NATIONAL HISTORY OF THE HEBREW NATION

The **BIBLE** *Graphically Presented*

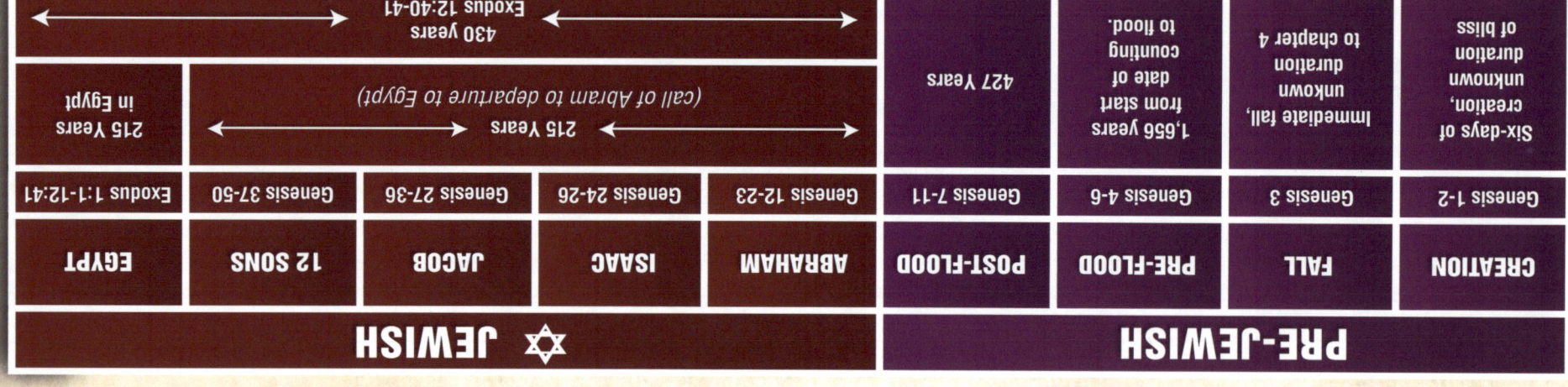

PRE-JEWISH				JEWISH 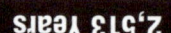				
CREATION	FALL	PRE-FLOOD	POST-FLOOD	ABRAHAM	ISAAC	JACOB	12 SONS	EGYPT
Genesis 1-2	Genesis 3	Genesis 4-6	Genesis 7-11	Genesis 12-23	Genesis 24-26	Genesis 27-36	Genesis 37-50	Exodus 1:1-12:41
Six-days of creation, unknown duration of bliss	Immediate fall, unknown duration to chapter 4	1,656 years from start date of counting to flood.	427 years	215 years (call of Abram to departure to Egypt)				215 Years in Egypt
				430 years Exodus 12:40-41				

unknown duration ← → **2,513 Years** ← →

- God created a perfect world out of nothing
- Man chose to reject God and suffer the consequences
- God destroyed the earth because Satan sought to block the plan for a Savior
- The earth was populated and nations were established
- God chose one man through whom He would work
- God pictured redemption through sacrifice
- God displayed His sovereign choice
- God developed a family into a clan
- God developed a clan into a nation

Description

Genesis 1–Exodus 12:41 describes the work of God before the birth of the Hebrew nation. The period of time covered in Genesis 1-3 is of unknown duration. The remaining time is 2,513 years, a time in which God called Abram and developed the nation that would be the focus of His work through the remainder of the Hebrew Scriptures. The chronology is gleaned through computation of ages given in the genealogies.

Notes

THE NATIONAL HISTORY OF THE HEBREW NATION

The BIBLE *Graphically Presented*

THEOCRACY ─ MONARCHY

WILDERNESS	CONQUEST	JUDGES	UNITED MONARCHY		
Moses	Joshua	12 Judges	Saul	David	Solomon
Numbers 1-36	Joshua 1-24	Judges 1-21	1 Sam. 8:1-31:13	2 Sam. 1:1 – 1 Kings 2:11	1 Kings 2:12-11:43

480 Years – 1 Kings 6:1

40 Years	Approx 356 Years		Approx 84 years to Solomon's 4th Year		
THE LAW	THE LAND	THE LIBERTY	THE LEGISLATION		
Everyone 20 years old and older dies. God establishes His rule.	Joshua conquers and divides the land among the 12 tribes.	THE CYCLE OF SIN IN JUDGES — Israel serves the Lord; Israel falls into sin & idolatry; Israel is enslaved; Israel cries out to the Lord; Israel is delivered	Saul is chosen by man and for man — this is a total rejection of God.	David is chosen by God and for God and becomes foundational in the coming Kingdom of God.	Solomon builds the temple in the 4th year of his reign.

In those days there was no king in Israel – Judges 21:25 | *Appoint a king... to judge us – 1 Samuel 8:5*

10

Description

With the giving of the Law at Mt. Sinai, the Hebrew nation was born. After 40 years of wilderness wanderings, the land was conquered and the people lived in liberty. This liberty led to ruin when it became libertine rather than liberty. The people demanded a king and abandoned the theocracy.

Notes

___
___
___
___
___
___
___
___
___

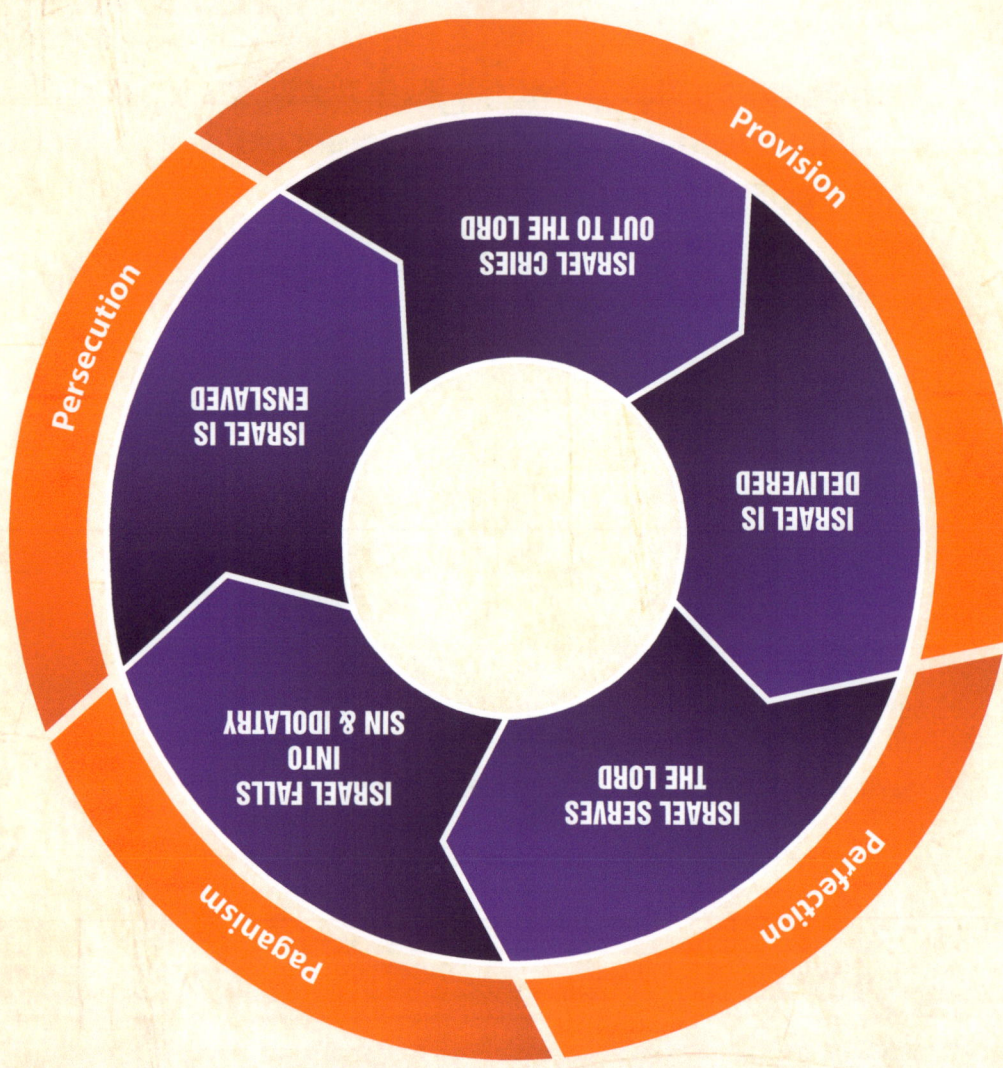

Description

The problem of Israel was based in forgetfulness. Regular observances of spiritual and civic significance are necessary to a long memory, and Israel was failing to have the observances instructed in the Law. The problem of forgetfulness led to a culture of paganism. Paganism: Judges 2:11-13, Persecution: Judges 2:14-15, Provision: Judges 2:16, Perpetual cycle: Judges 2:17-20.

Notes

___

___

___

___

___

___

___

THE DIVIDED KINGDOM AND BEYOND

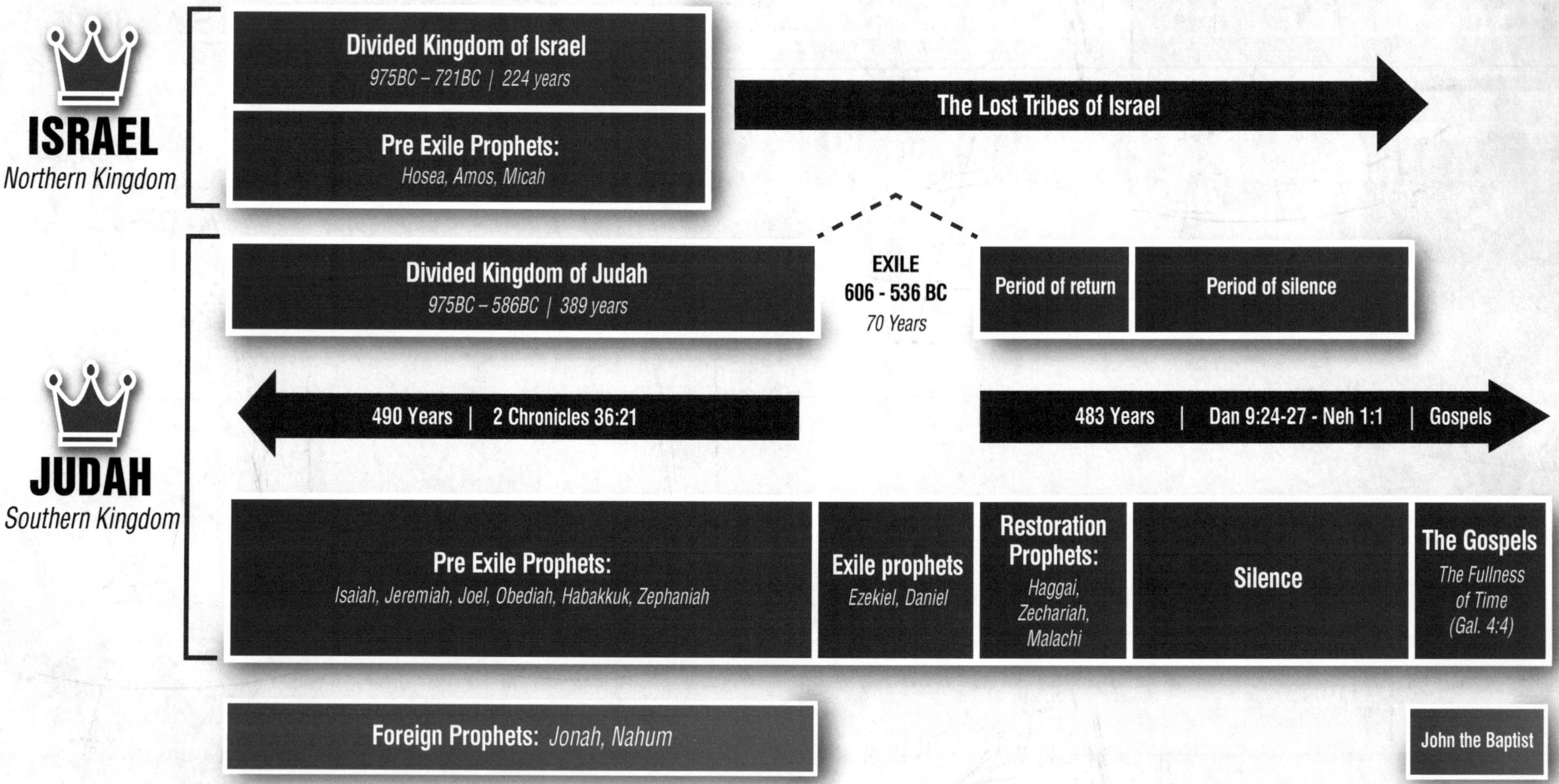

The Bible Graphically Presented

JUDAH — Southern Kingdom

Foreign Prophets: Jonah, Nahum

Pre Exile Prophets: Isaiah, Jeremiah, Joel, Obadiah, Habakkuk, Zephaniah

Exile prophets: Ezekiel, Daniel

Restoration Prophets: Haggai, Zechariah, Malachi

Silence

The Gospels — The Fullness of Time (Gal. 4:4)

John the Baptist

← 490 Years | 2 Chronicles 36:21
← 483 Years | Dan 9:24-27 - Neh 1:1 | Gospels

Divided Kingdom of Judah — 975BC – 586BC | 389 years

EXILE 606 - 536 BC — 70 Years

Period of return | Period of silence

ISRAEL — Northern Kingdom

Divided Kingdom of Israel — 975BC – 721BC | 224 years

Pre Exile Prophets: Hosea, Amos, Micah

← The Lost Tribes of Israel

Description

The period of the divided kingdom, exile and return is one of the most important periods of Israel's history. The experiences of this period shaped Israel in ways that affect the Jewish people to this day. The "lost tribes" were scattered and only scantly returned in Biblical times, and in greater numbers in modern times. These tribes were, in large part, the Jewish people who were scattered abroad in the days of the New Testament epistles. The Judeans were prominent in Jesus' day, as prophesied in Genesis 49:10. Modern Israel is composed of all 12 tribes, though tribal identity was largely lost with the destruction of the Temple in 70 AD.

Notes

_____

_____

_____

_____

_____

_____

THE DIVIDED KINGDOM

NORTHERN KINGDOM – ISRAEL

10 Tribes: Reuben, Simeon, Dan, Naphtali, Gad, Asher, Issachar, Zebulun, Ephraim, Manasseh

Capital: Samaria

Period: 931 – 722 BC (224 years)

Rulers: 19 Kings and nine dynasties

Fall: Despite God's warning (2 Kings 17:13-18), Israel remains disobedient and so the Kingdom was conquered by the Assyrians.

Assyrian Captivity

SOUTHERN KINGDOM – JUDAH

10 Tribes: Judah, Benjamin

Capital: Jerusalem

Period: 931 – 586 BC (389 years)

Rulers: 20 Kings and one dynasty (Davidic)

Fall: Judah served under the Babylonians from 606 BC until the destruction of Jerusalem and the end of the Kingdom of Judah in 586 BC.

Babylonic Captivity

Description

Understanding the period of the divided kingdom will help you comprehend many of the prophets and the nature of the Hebrew nation in Jesus' time. The Northern Kingdom was always in disobedience to God (having broken from the Davidic covenant) and never had a good king. The Southern Kingdom was randomly in obedience to God and had a few good kings, interspersed with many who did evil.

Notes

CAPTIVITY AND RETURN

CAPTIVITY

606 BC
Many of the king's family were taken to Babylon. Daniel was among these captives.

596 BC
A second group was taken captive in 596 BC, made up of priests and skilled craftsman. Ezekiel was among this group.

586 BC
Nebuchadnezzar destroyed the city and Solomon's temple, taking all but the poor and sick as captives to Babylon.

70 YEARS OF EXILE
606 – 536 BC

539 BC
The Babylonian Empire was conquered by the Medes and the Persians. Soon afterward, Cyrus the Great gave the Jews permission to return to their homeland and permission to rebuild the temple (2 Chron. 36:22-23, Ezra 1:1-4).

RETURN

536 BC
The first group of captives returned, led by Zerubbabel, who was a descendant of King David. Zerubbabel rebuilt the temple, completed in 516. 49,697 people returned.
Ezra 1 - 6

458 BC
The second group of Jews returned, led by Ezra, a scribe of God's law. Ezra reinstated the temple worship. 1,758 people returned.
Ezra 7 - 10

444 BC
The third group returned led by Nehemiah, who rebuilt the walls of Jerusalem in 52 days.
Nehemiah 1-13

Description

The exile and return made indelible marks on the Hebrew nation. God had prophesied that Cyrus would be the one to make the decree to allow the Jews to return to Jerusalem. This prophecy is found in Isaiah 44:28, almost 200 years before the event took place. God had also revealed to Daniel that the decree to rebuild the city would be the starting point for the countdown to Messiah, given in Daniel 9:24-27.

Notes

DANIEL'S VISION OF WORLD HISTORY

The **BIBLE** *Graphically Presented*

DANIEL 2	EMPIRE	PERIOD	DANIEL 7	DANIEL 8
	**Gold** Babylonian Empire	612 – 538 B.C.		
	Silver Medo-Persian Empire	538 – 330 B.C.		
	Bronze Greek Empire	330 – 63 B.C.		
	Iron Roman Empire	63 B.C. –		
	Iron and Clay Revived Roman Empire	After the rapture		

Description

Daniel's vision of world history is fundamental to our understanding of world events in the past and in the future. This revelation, received 2,600 years ago, has been proven accurate in every detail. We can rest assured that the future aspects of the vision will be equally fulfilled in accuracy. This gives us insight into the future origins and reign of the Antichrist.

Notes

THE CHRONOLOGICAL OLD TESTAMENT

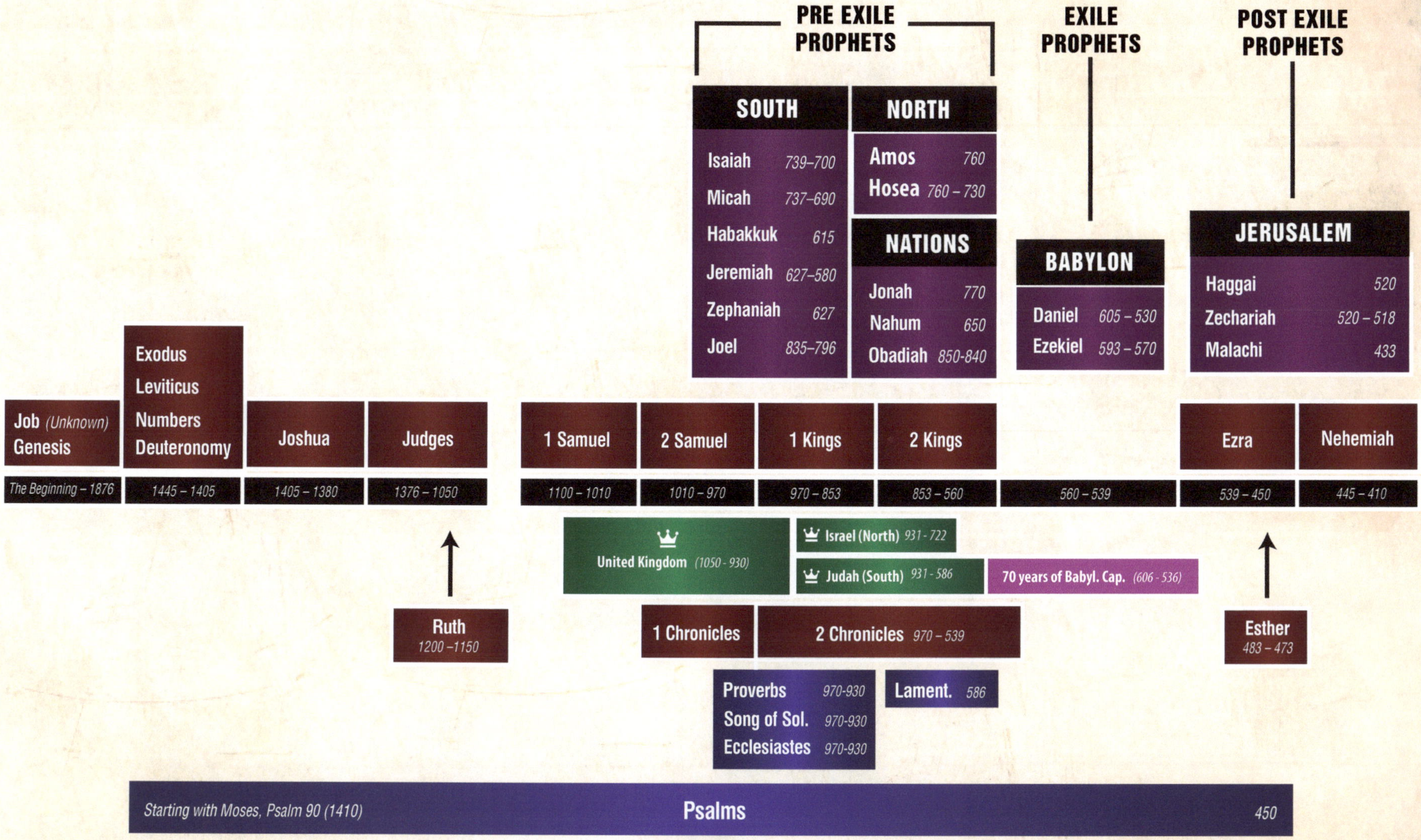

The BIBLE Graphically Presented

22

Psalms — Starting with Moses, Psalm 90 (1410) — 450

	Proverbs 970-930	
	Song of Sol. 970-930	
	Ecclesiastes 970-930	
Lament. 586		
Esther 483-473	1 Chronicles	2 Chronicles 970-539
	Ruth 1200-1150	

70 years of Babyl. Cap. (606-536)
Judah (South) 931-586
Israel (North) 931-722
United Kingdom (1050-930)

Genesis	Exodus Leviticus Numbers Deuteronomy	Joshua	Judges	1 Samuel	2 Samuel	1 Kings	2 Kings	Ezra	Nehemiah
The Beginning – 1876 Job (Unknown)	1445-1405	1405-1380	1376-1050	1100-1010	1010-970	970-853	853-560	560-539	539-450	445-410

SOUTH
- Isaiah 739-700
- Micah 737-690
- Habakkuk 615
- Jeremiah 627-580
- Zephaniah 627
- Joel 835-796

NORTH
- Amos 760
- Hosea 760-730
- Jonah 770
- Nahum 650
- Obadiah 850-840

PRE EXILE PROPHETS

BABYLON
- Daniel 605-530
- Ezekiel 593-570

EXILE PROPHETS

JERUSALEM
- Haggai 520
- Zechariah 520-518
- Malachi 433

POST EXILE PROPHETS

Description

Understanding the chronological layout of the Hebrew Scriptures is very helpful to understanding the message of God through the dispensations. Our 39 books we call the Old Testament are laid out in rough chronological order through the book of Nehemiah. The prophetic books, which took place at the same time period discussed in the historical books of 1 Samuel – Nehemiah, can be overlaid on these chronologies in order to get the complete picture of God's work.

Notes

BETWEEN THE TESTAMENTS

The Bible Graphically Presented

The Persian Empire 550-330BC	**The Greek Empire** 330-164BC	**The Macabees (Hasmoneans)** 164-63BC	**The Roman Empire** 63BC - New Testament
Daniel 2:39	Daniel 8:5-8, 20-22		Daniel 2:40

Cyrus the Great, Darius, Xerxes, Artaxerxes	Alexander the Great, Antiochus Ephiphenes	A priestly family, Mattathias and his five sons	The Caesars in Rome, Herod the Great in Israel
Return to Israel and Restoration of Jerusalem	Jerusalem spared under Alexander, Destroyed under Antiochus Ephiphenes	Temple Rededicated	Magnificent rebuilding of the Temple as well as other landmarks of Israel

Description

From the point of the return of the Babylonian captives through the opening of the New Testament, the Hebrew nation was in its homeland but rarely independent and sovereign. The flow of history was pre-recorded by Daniel in both Daniel 2, 7 and 8.

Notes

The New Testament

THE PRESENTATION OF THE KING AND HIS KINGDOM

The Bible Graphically Presented

BIRTH & FLIGHT TO EGYPT	CHILDHOOD TO 30 YEARS	THE KINGDOM PRESENTED		THE KING REJECTED			THE KINGDOM OFFERED
The "fullness of time" – Genesis 3:15 comes to fruition	Years of silence	Announced by John the Baptist	Announced by Jesus	Announced by Apostles	Requirement: Repentance	Rejection of Jesus: blasphemer	Removal of Jesus: Crucifixion for insurrection	All prophetic requirements for the Kingdom have been fulfilled, now Israel must accept her King
		"Repent, the Kingdom is at Hand." Matt 3:2	"Repent, the Kingdom is at hand." Matt 4:17	Preach, saying 'The Kingdom is at hand.' Matt 10:7	Matthew 3:2	Matthew 26:63-65	Matthew 27:37	Acts 1-8

30 Years — **3 Years** — **11 Years**

Description

When Jesus came as Messiah, He did not fulfill every aspect of His plan for the world. Dying, He rose again, only to ascend to heaven, from where He will return to establish the promised Kingdom and do what the first Adam could not do: take dominion of all the created order. This means that Jesus must return to complete His ultimate mission. One of the first signs of His return is the broad-based promise of a re-established Hebrew nation. From here, the prophetic word narrows the focus until there will be no doubt that every prophecy has been fulfilled and Christ will return.

Notes

_____

_____

_____

_____

_____

_____

_____

HAS THE KINGDOM ARRIVED?

> *The Kingdom of God, the redemptive activity and power of God, is working in the world today through the Church of Jesus Christ.*
> **George Eldon Ladd**

OLD TESTAMENT PROPHETS	JOHN THE BAPTIST	JESUS	APOSTLES	APOCALYPSE
Daniel 2:44	ἤγγικω: the occurrence of a point of time close to a subsequent point of time—"to approach, to come near, to approximate."		Acts 1:5	Rev. 12:10

> *The Kingdom of God is future, fraternal, and physical.*
> **Randy White**

30

Description

While the predominant theological persuasion today is that the kingdom of God was established somewhere in Jesus' life or shortly thereafter, this position is not supported by Scripture. The kingdom is not present, it is not the church, and it is not a spiritual kingdom within your heart. Rather, the Bible presents the kingdom as future, fraternal (related to Israel), and physical.

Notes

PREREQUISITES TO THE KINGDOM OF GOD

PROPHECIES THAT MUST BE FULFILLED BEFORE THE KINGDOM CAN BE OFFERED

Messiah born in Bethlehem	Micah 2:4
Messiah had to give evidence of His authority	Luke 4:18
Messiah had to be crucified	Psalm 22:16-18, Daniel 9:26
Messiah's crucifixion had to be a sin offering, appointed by God	Isaiah 53:10, Acts 2:22-23
Messiah had to be buried in the tomb of a rich man	Isaiah 53:9
Messiah had to be resurrected	Psalm 16:10 (defined as Messianic in Acts 2:10)
Messiah had to ascend to heaven	Psalm 110:1
The Holy Spirit had to be given	Joel 2:28-29

Without the fulfillment of these prophecies prior to the establishment of the Kingdom, the Hebrew Scriptures would have been found to be false.

Description

The demand of Hebrew prophecy is an "all or nothing" demand. Every prophecy must be fulfilled or the prophet must be rejected. If any of the prophecies of Messiah's birth, life, death, burial, resurrection or ascension had not been fulfilled, the Hebrew Scriptures would have been inaccurate. Therefore, all of these had to be fulfilled prior to any possible offer and acceptance of the Kingdom. An offer before these prophecies had been fulfilled would not have been bona fide.

Notes

_____
_____
_____
_____
_____
_____
_____

THE FALL OF ISRAEL AND THE RISE OF THE CHURCH
The Book of Acts

ASSEMBLY OF JEWISH BELIEVERS
33-44 A.D.
Led by Peter

THE CHURCH-AGE ASSEMBLY
44-66 AD
Assembly of Jewish Believers led by James
Gentile Assembly led by Paul

Watching, 1:1-11		
Waiting, 1:12-26	Acts 3-4 — Growth (Proclamation, Partnership, Persecution)	
Witnessing, 2:1-47		
	Internal Threat 5:1-16	1st Missionary Journey 13:1-15:35	46-50 AD
	External Threat 5:17-42	2nd Missionary Journey 15:36-18:22	50-52 AD
	Internal Threat 6:1-7	3rd Missionary Journey 18:23-21:16	52-57 AD
	External Threat 6:8-8:3	Imprisoned in Jerusalem: 21:17-23:35	57 AD
	Divided but not conquered 8:4-11:30	Imprisoned in Caesarea 24-26	57-59 AD
	The end of the Jerusalem Era 12:1-25	Imprisoned in Rome 27-28	59-66 AD

The Bible Graphically Presented

Description

Understanding the book of Acts is fundamental to understanding the remainder of the New Testament. The book of Acts is not as much about the birth and growth of the church as it is an explanation of the fall of Israel from the focus of God's work and the subsequent rise of a predominantly Gentile body that was not under the law but under grace.

Notes

_____
_____
_____
_____
_____
_____
_____
_____

THE CHRONOLOGICAL NEW TESTAMENT

JERUSALEM
45-50

- James — 45-48
- Galatians — 48
- Matthew — 50

SCATTERING
50-60

- 1 & 2 Thes. — 50-54
- 1 Cor. — 54-55
- 2 Cor. — 56-57
- Mark — 57-59
- Romans — 57-58
- Luke — 58-60

GROWING THREAT
60-64

- Ephesians — 60
- Colossians — 60
- Philippians — 60
- Philemon — 60
- 1,2,3 John — 60-62
- Acts — 60-62
- 1 Timothy — 63-66
- Titus — 63-66
- 1 Peter — 64

SEVERE PERSECUTION
64-96

- 2 Peter — 64-68
- 2 Timothy — 67
- Jude — 67-80
- Hebrews — 68-69
- John — 85-95
- Revelation — 95-96

The **BIBLE** *Graphically Presented*

Description

The New Testament is completely written in the Greek language. It is written partly to Jews and under the Jewish law and partly to the church free from the law. Only by rightly dividing the word of truth can proper application be made. When you apply to the church that which is directed toward Israel, the result is legalism and its offspring, pharisaical religious practice.

Notes

The New Testament
The Book of Revelation

COMPARISON OF REVELATION SEALS WITH MATTHEW 24

MATTHEW 24 | SEALS OF REVELATION

Matthew 24		Seals of Revelation
Matthew 24:4-5	↔	First seal (Rev. 6:1-2)
Matthew 24:6-7	↔	Second, third and fourth seals (Rev. 6:3-8)
Matthew 24:8-28	↔	Fifth seal (Rev. 6:9-11)
Matthew 24:29-30 (Also Joel 2:28,31)	↔	Sixth seal (Rev. 6:12-17)
Matthew 24:31-51	↔	Sealing of the 144,000 (Rev. 7:1 – 19:21)

70th Week of Daniel

The BIBLE Graphically Presented

Description

When studied closely, the description of the end times given by Jesus on the Mount of Olives harmonizes perfectly with the seven seals of the book of Revelation. Any student who works to harmonize prophecy will always be able to do so, with great insight into the past, present and future.

Notes

THE CHURCHES OF REVELATION | INTERPRETIVE VIEWS
Historic View

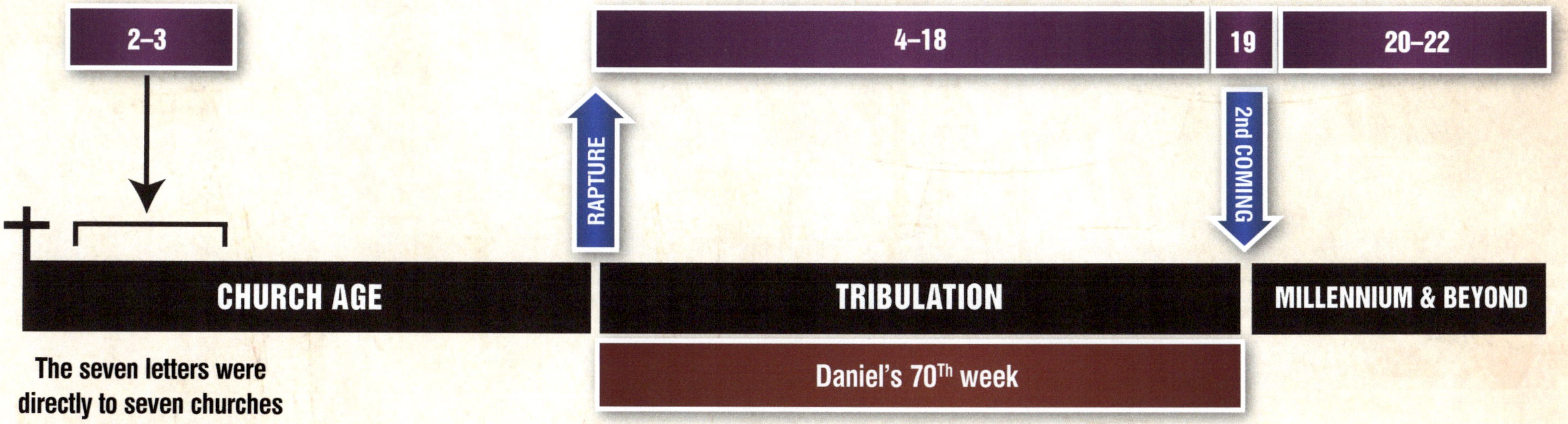

CHURCH AGE | **TRIBULATION** | **MILLENNIUM & BEYOND**

Daniel's 70th week

RAPTURE → | ← 2nd COMING

2–3 | 4–18 | 19 | 20–22

The seven letters were directly to seven churches of Asia Minor and the interpretation is to them alone, with only secondary interpretation beyond.

Description

The matter of the interpretation of the seven churches can make significant impact on application for today. This historic view takes a preterist approach to Revelation 2-3, even if it does not take such an approach beyond these chapters. In this historic view, one would not make direct application of the letters to churches today.

Notes

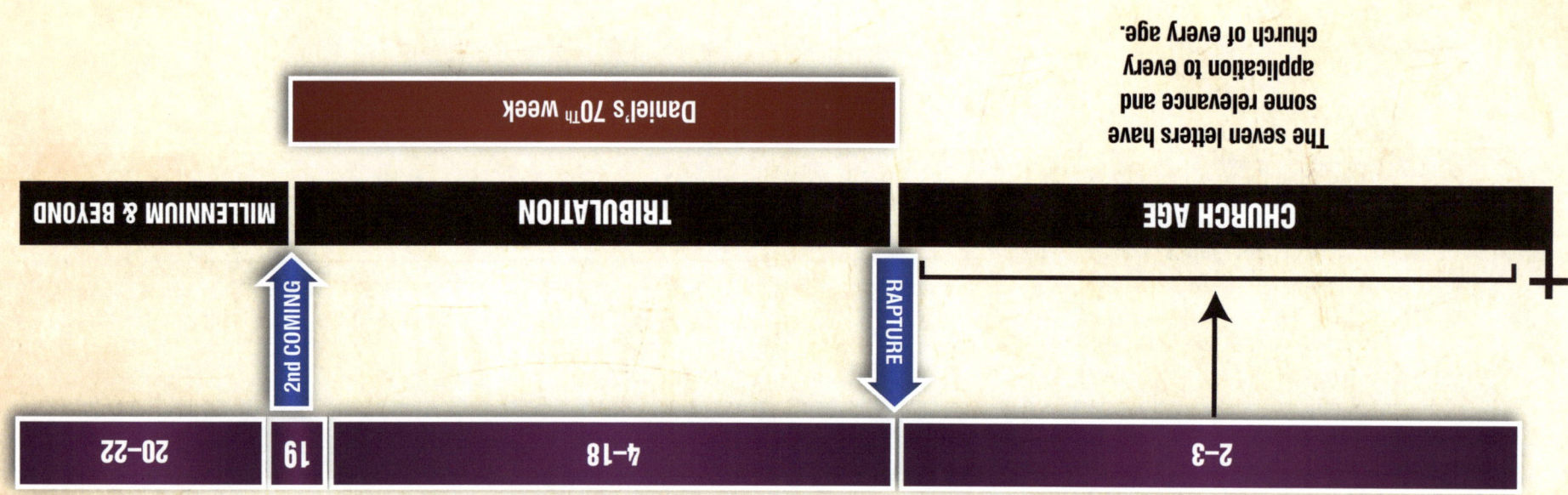

Description

The dynamic and prophetic view says that the letters to the churches have relevance in every age. The prophetic side of this view is a view of implicit prophecy within the letters. This view has been held by many classic dispensational teachers. In this view, the resemblance of remarks to the seven churches to the events of church history are noted. The rapture is seen to be at Revelation 4:1, after which point the word church does not appear. In this view, Revelation 4-22 is seen as future.

Notes

THE CHURCHES OF REVELATION | INTERPRETIVE VIEWS
Futurist View

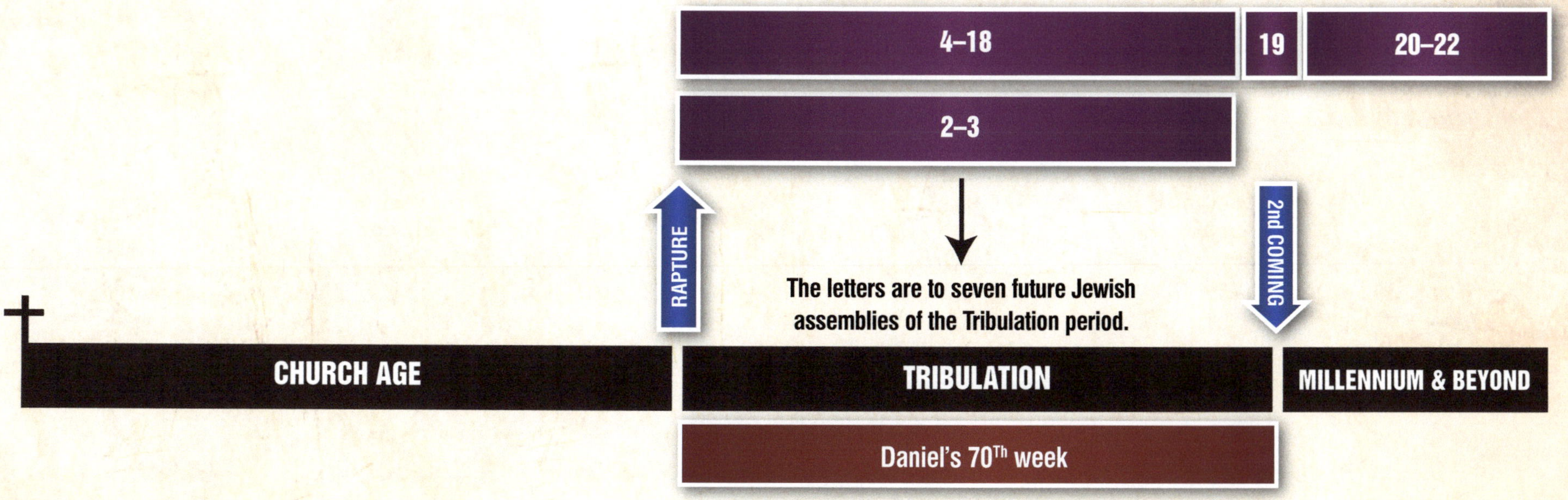

CHURCH AGE — **TRIBULATION** — **MILLENNIUM & BEYOND**

Daniel's 70th week

RAPTURE

2nd COMING

The letters are to seven future Jewish assemblies of the Tribulation period.

2–3

4–18 | 19 | 20–22

Description

The futurist view recognizes some problems with interpretation of the letters to the seven churches during the dispensation of grace and believes that the seven churches are actually Jewish assemblies that will be actual and real, but are yet future. The instructions are to the Jews in these assemblies, some of whom will recognize Jesus as Messiah and will live faithfully for him.

Notes

AN ALTERNATE CHRONOLOGY OF THE BOOK OF REVELATION

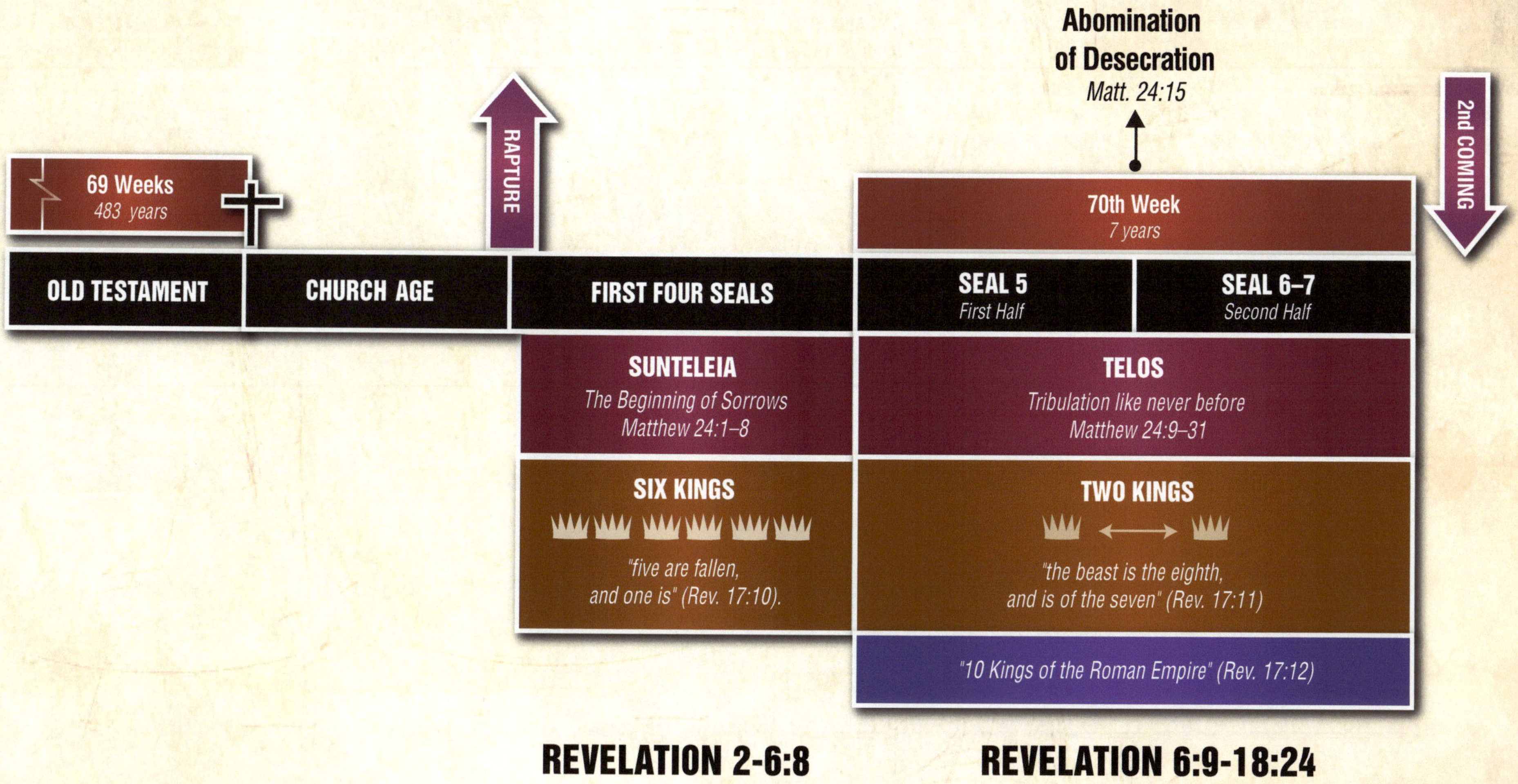

The BIBLE Graphically Presented

REVELATION 2-6:8

REVELATION 6:9-18:24

OLD TESTAMENT — 69 Weeks, 483 years

CHURCH AGE

RAPTURE

FIRST FOUR SEALS

SUNTELEIA — The Beginning of Sorrows, Matthew 24:1-8

SIX KINGS — "five are fallen, and one is" (Rev. 17:10).

70th Week — 7 years

SEAL 5 — First Half

SEAL 6-7 — Second Half

TELOS — Tribulation like never before, Matthew 24:9-31

TWO KINGS — "the beast is the eighth, and is of the seven" (Rev. 17:11).

"10 kings of the Roman Empire" (Rev. 17:12)

Abomination of Desecration Matt. 24:15

2nd COMING

48

Description

Almost all dispensational chronologies of the book of Revelation have the commencement of the 70th Week of Daniel with the first seal. This alternate chronology puts the first four seals into a "beginning of sorrows" time-period of unknown duration (but not more than a lifespan). The tribulation of seven years then begins with Revelation 6:9. This is done to harmonize the Olivet Discourse of Matthew 24 with the book of Revelation.

Notes

Theology

Theology
General

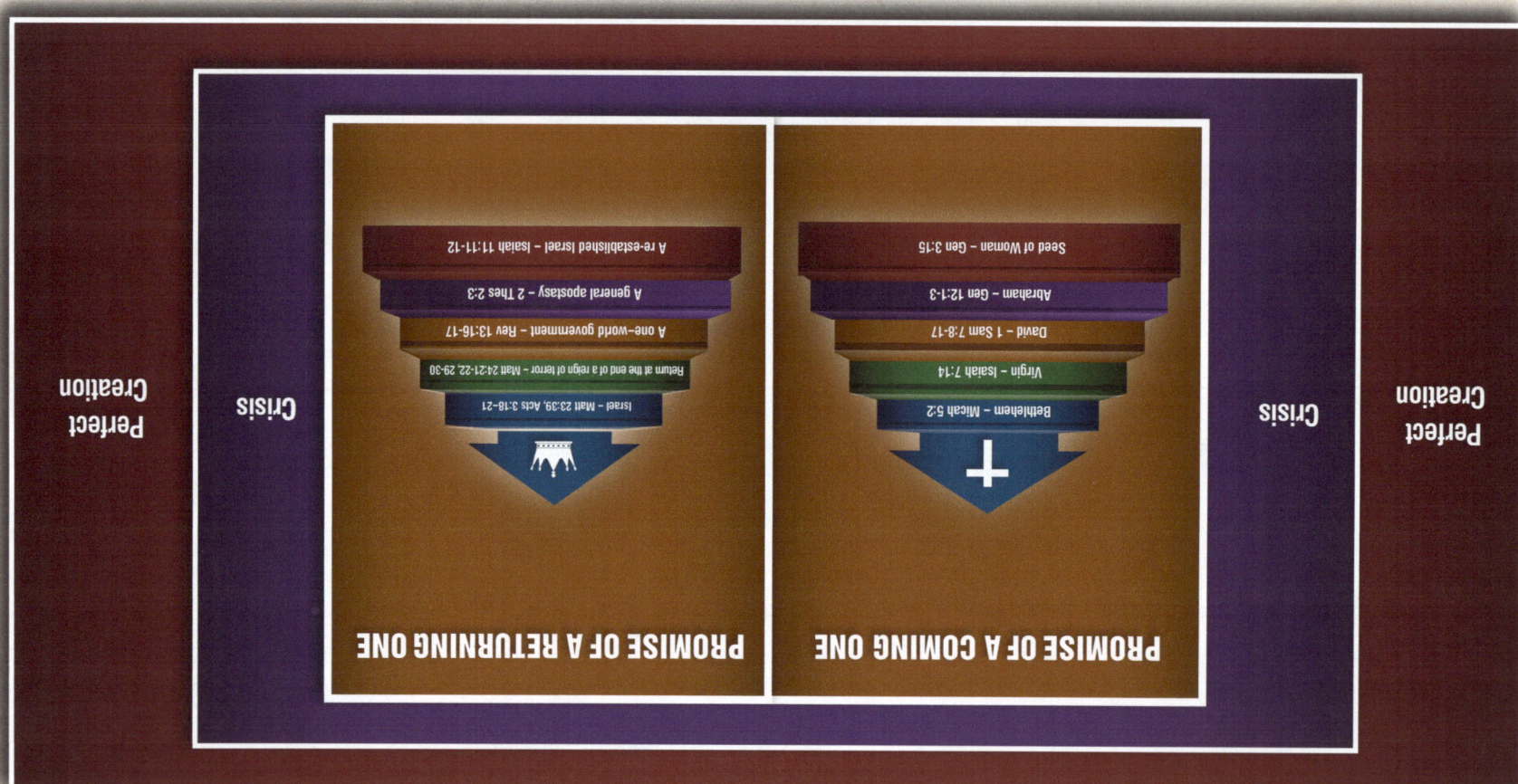

Description

God created a perfect world. At the end of is creative work, the Lord proclaimed it "very good" (Genesis 1:31). It wasn't long, however, until a crisis began, one that has encompassed all of creation to this day. Within this crisis God promised a Redeemer. That Promised One has come and has become the propitiation of the sins of all the world, but ascended to heaven before perfecting the created order again. Today there is a promise of His return, but before creation is perfected once again, there will be another crisis, which is Biblically called, "the Day of the Lord."

Notes

Description

The crisis of sin brought about the curse, which introduced death and suffering into the world. While God could have allowed Adam and Eve and their offspring to simply die and the created order to disintegrate, this would not have been to His glory. So God made the promise of a Redeemer. This promise is given a very broad base in Genesis 3:15, but future prophecies and revelations would pinpoint the coming Redeemer with laser-focused accuracy.

Notes

The BIBLE Graphically Presented

PROMISE OF A RETURNING ONE

- A re-established Israel – Isaiah 11:11-12
- A general apostasy – 2 Thes 2:3
- A one-world government – Rev 13:16-17
- Return at the end of a reign of terror – Matt 24:21-22, 29-30
- Israel – Matt 23:39, Acts 3:18-21

Description

When Jesus came as Messiah, he did not complete his mission. Dying, he rose again, only to ascend to heaven before establishing the promised Kingdom and doing what the first Adam could not do: take dominion of all the created order. This means that Jesus must return to complete his mission. One of the first signs of his return is the broad-based promise of a re-established Hebrew nation. From here, the prophetic word narrows the focus until there will be no doubt that every prophecy has been fulfilled and Christ will return.

Notes

Description

Biblical covenants are important to understanding God's dispensational work in the world. Biblical covenants are not the same as the "theological covenants" assumed by "Covenant" Theology. This box shows that the Noahic and Abrahamic covenants extend to this day, while the Mosaic covenant ceased at the dispensation of grace. The Davidic covenant has been put on hold and will later re-emerge, after this dispensation is complete. The New Covenant will be fulfilled within the future fulfillment of the davidic covenant.

Notes

The BIBLE Graphically Presented

THE ORIGIN OF EVIL
Three Views

| Eternity Past | God Created the Heavens and the Earth | It was very good |

1 PRE-BEGINNING THEORY

The pre-beginning theory says that a fallen Satan already existed before "the beginning" of Genesis 1:1. This idea is erroneously based on Nehemiah 9:6, and maintains that all of the angels were, in fact, created before this time.

2 GAP THEORY

The gap theory says that Satan and the evil angels fell between Genesis 1:1 and 1:2. Many older dispensationalists taught that there was a gap in between those verses, during which a catastrophe took place. This view is erroneously built on the assumption that—although God created a perfect world—it later became "without form and void" (Gen. 1:2).

3 GARDEN THEORY

The garden theory simply states that somewhere between Genesis 2 and 3 Satan rebelled against God and was cast down to the earth in the from of a serpent. This is the only explanation that fits together with this basic statement in Genesis 1:31: "And God saw every thing that he had made, and, behold, it was very good…"

62

Description

The origin of evil has been a topic of discussion for as long as theologians have gathered to discuss! While the Bible only gives glimpses into the timing of the rebellion and fall of Satan, the most theologically accurate time that fits the Biblical text is that these events took place after the placement of Adam and Eve in the Garden.

Notes

THE WORK OF SATAN

LUCIFER

In Genesis he is only known as the "serpent." Later he is "the adversary." His pre-fall name was Lucifer, an angel of light, with unknown duties. The name comes from Latin. The Hebrew is helel, the "morning star."

REBELLION
Lucifer desired to have the place of God and thus was cast from heaven and given an ultimate promise of destruction in Genesis 3:15.

Isaiah 14:12-15

CURRENT WORK
Satan is active in the world today as "the god of this world" and is working to "devour" whom he may. He is still under the limits of our sovereign God.

2 Cor. 4:4, 1 Peter 5:8

FUTURE FALL
Though Satan is the "accuser of the brethren" today, he will be removed from any access to heaven in the future.

Job 1:6-8, Rev. 12:7-9

ULTIMATE DEMISE
Satan will be cast into the Lake of Fire, which has been prepared especially for him.

Rev. 20:10

Description

The work of Satan is the ultimate "anti-Christ" work. Satan is known as the serpent, the devil, Satan, Lucifer, the dragon and more. His ultimate goal is to avoid the defeat prophesied in Genesis 3:15, thus his greatest work is to destroy the ability of the Messiah to fulfill prophecy.

Notes

MILLENNIAL VIEWS
Postmillennialism

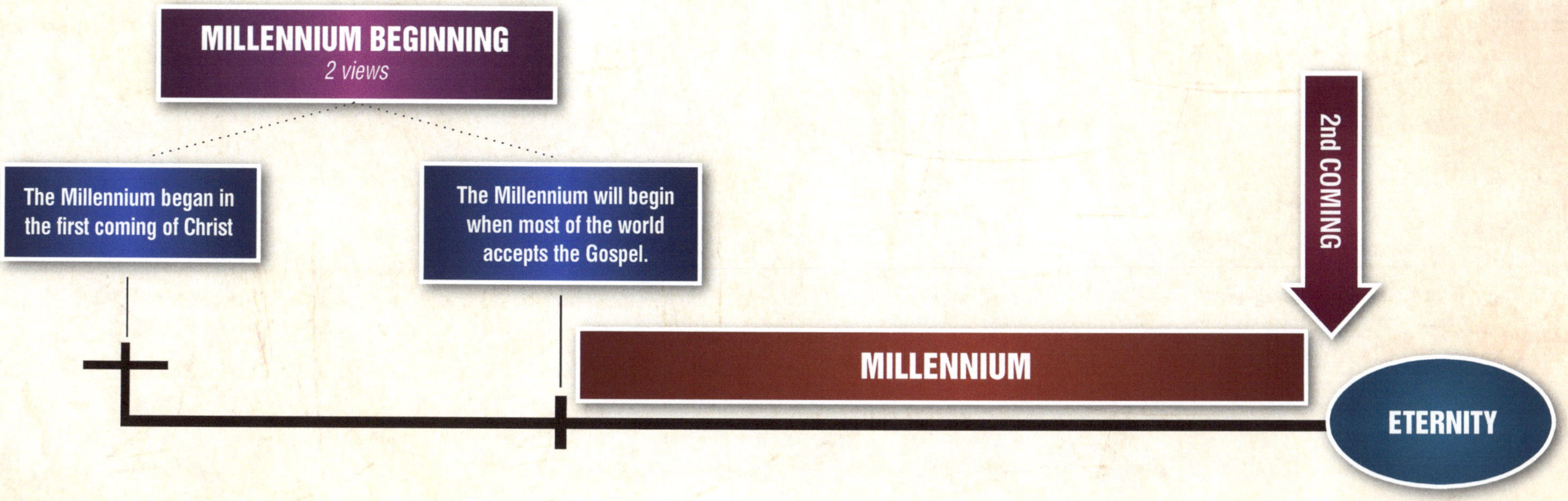

ETERNITY

MILLENNIUM

2nd COMING

MILLENNIUM BEGINNING — *2 views*

- The Millennium will begin when most of the world accepts the Gospel.
- The Millennium began in the first coming of Christ.

The Bible Graphically Presented

Description

Postmillennialism takes a spiritualized view of the Kingdom of God and the millennium. It envisions a world that is increasingly Christian in belief and behavior. The view was very popular in the industrial revolution, then died out with the World Wars. It has made a resurgence in the form of Dominionism and Restorationism.

Notes

MILLENNIAL VIEWS
Amillennialism

ETERNITY

MILLENNIUM
unknown duration

1,000 years = symbolic number

2nd COMING

BEGINNING MILLENNIUM
First Coming

The **BIBLE** *Graphically Presented*

Description

Amillennialism is a cousin to postmillennialism in that it spiritualizes the Kingdom of God and the Millennium. Amillennialism does not distinguish between Israel and the church. Amillennialism is held by the Roman Catholic Church as well as many adherents of Reformed theology, especially those in mainline protestant denominations. For the amillennialist, there is no tribulation and the events of the book of Revelation are either spiritualized or seen as having already occurred.

Notes

MILLENNIAL VIEWS
Historic Premillennialism

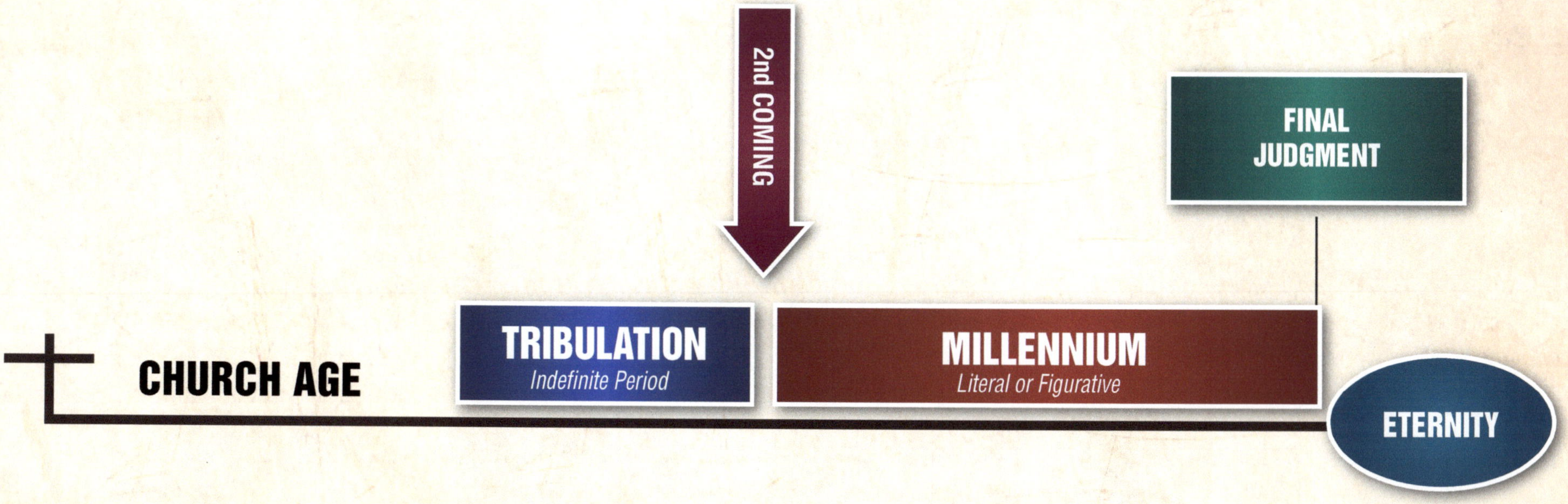

CHURCH AGE

TRIBULATION — Indefinite Period

MILLENNIUM — Literal or Figurative

2nd COMING

FINAL JUDGMENT

ETERNITY

70

The Bible Graphically Presented

Description

This position is called "historic" because it is claimed that the premillennialists of history held to this type of premillennialism. It is premillennial because it teaches the return of Jesus Christ prior to the establishment of the millennial Kingdom of God. Since it does not believe in a rapture prior to the tribulation, it is sometimes called "post-tribulational premillennialism." Believing the church will be in the tribulation, this position leans toward some degree of Calvinism since the church is considered by this group to be the "elect" that must endure the tribulation.

Notes

_____

_____

_____

_____

_____

_____

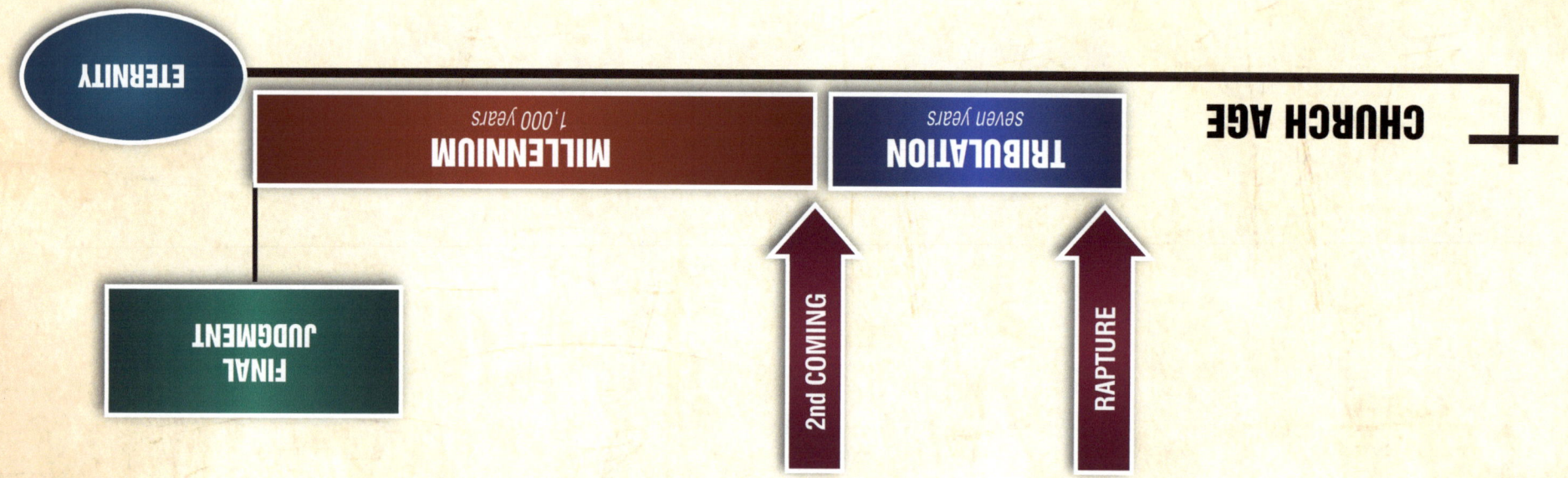

Description

This position is often seen as the definitive description of dispensational theology. However, it is actually a result of dispensationalism, which insists on reading Scripture in the same normal way that other descriptive works are read: literally, historically, grammatically, contextually. Because the dispensationalist is a literalist, a pre-tribulational rapture followed by a seven-year tribulation ending with the second coming of Christ and the establishment of His 1,000-year reign is a theological necessity. This is the only eschatological position that believes in a pre-tribulational rapture. The position has historic roots in non-Catholic groups of the Christian faith. With the predominance of Catholicism through history, this means that the teaching was inconspicuous until the rise of separatism and Biblically accurate streams of Christian faith in the 1700s and beyond.

Notes

FINDING THE DISPENSATIONS IN THE BIBLE

	Man with God:	Basic Content?	Where its found?
INNOCENCE	Full relationship	History	Gen. 1 - 2
CONSCIENCE	Use general revelation	History	Gen. 3-9
GOVERNMENT	General revelation plus specific punishment	History	Gen. 9-11
PROMISE	Come to God through Israel	History	Gen 12 – Ex 20
LAW	Come to God through the law	History	Ex 20 - Acts
GRACE	Come to God by grace through faith	Doctrinal	Acts - Jude
KINGDOM	Man with God	Revelation	Revelation

The **BIBLE** *Graphically Presented*

Description

A dispensation begins when a new revelation is given by God to man that changes man's fundamental requirements before God. The student of the Word must be careful not to apply requirements and blessings of one dispensation to the people of another dispensation unless the Scripture is explicit in its instruction to do so. Rightly dividing the word of truth is accomplished when we divide the dispensations. Almost all of what seems to be a contradiction in Scripture comes from the mixing of dispensations.

Notes

_____
_____
_____
_____
_____
_____
_____

Theology
From the Old Testament

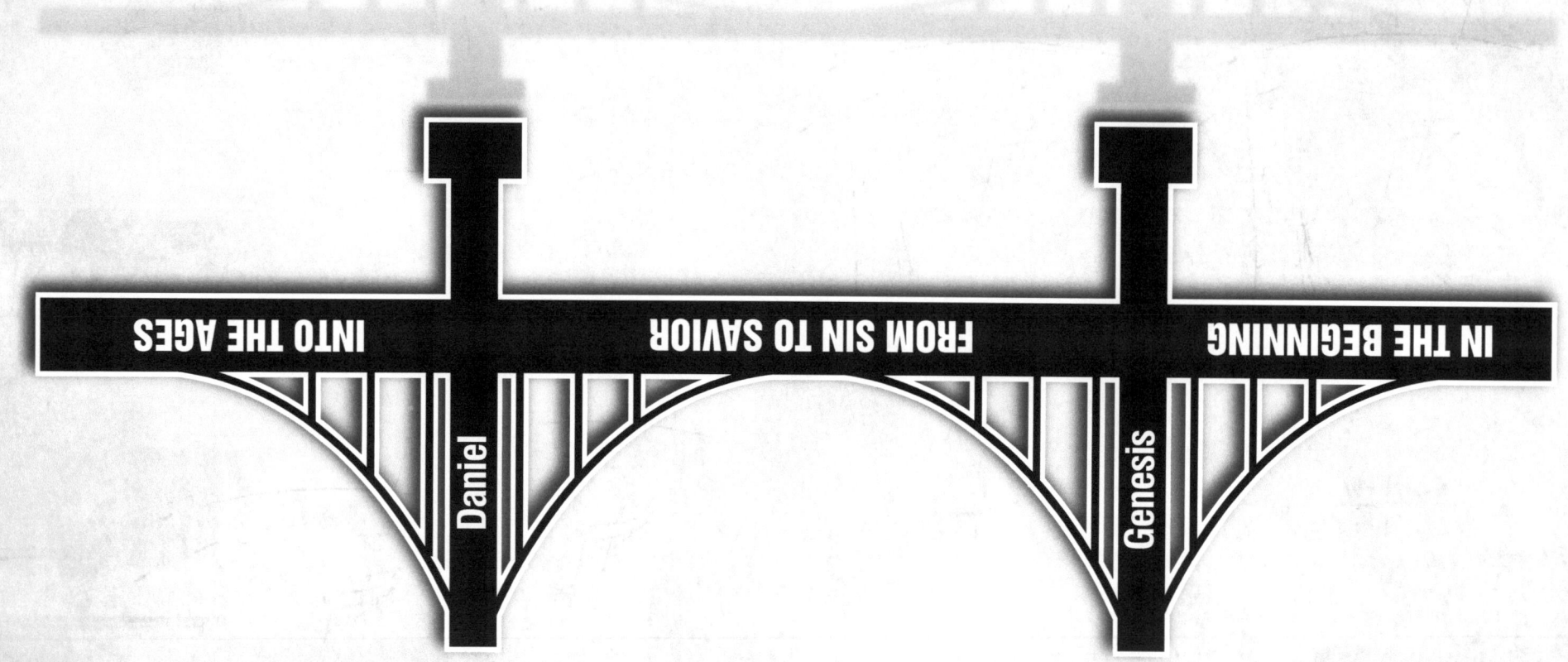

THE CHRONOLOGICAL SUSPENSION BRIDGE

IN THE BEGINNING — Genesis
FROM SIN TO SAVIOR
INTO THE AGES — Daniel

The Bible Graphically Presented

Description

All the weight of Biblical chronology rests upon the information and accuracy of Genesis and Daniel. It is no wonder that these two books have been attacked more than any other books in the Bible. The truthfulness of Genesis and Daniel are essential to understanding any kind of Biblical chronology and Biblical worldview.

Notes

THE TABLETS OF GENESIS

HEAVENS AND EARTH'S TABLET
Genesis 1:1–2:3

ADAM'S TABLET
Genesis 2:4–5:2

NOAH'S TABLET
Genesis 5:3–6:9

NOAH'S SONS' TABLET
Genesis 6:10–10:1

SHEM'S TABLET
Genesis 10:2–11:10

TERAH'S TABLET
Genesis 11:11–11:27

ISHMAEL & ISAAC'S TABLET
Genesis 11:28–25:19

JACOB & ESAU'S TABLET
Genesis 25:20–37:2

The **BIBLE** *Graphically Presented*

Description

The phrase, "These are the generations of..." is the key to understanding the origin of the book of Genesis. The statement is given as a summary of the previous verses. This means that Genesis 2:4–37:2 was written by eye-witnesses and compiled into a unit by Moses.

Notes

Theology
From the New Testament

The BIBLE Graphically Presented

PAUL AND THE 12 APOSTLES

TWELVE APOSTLES

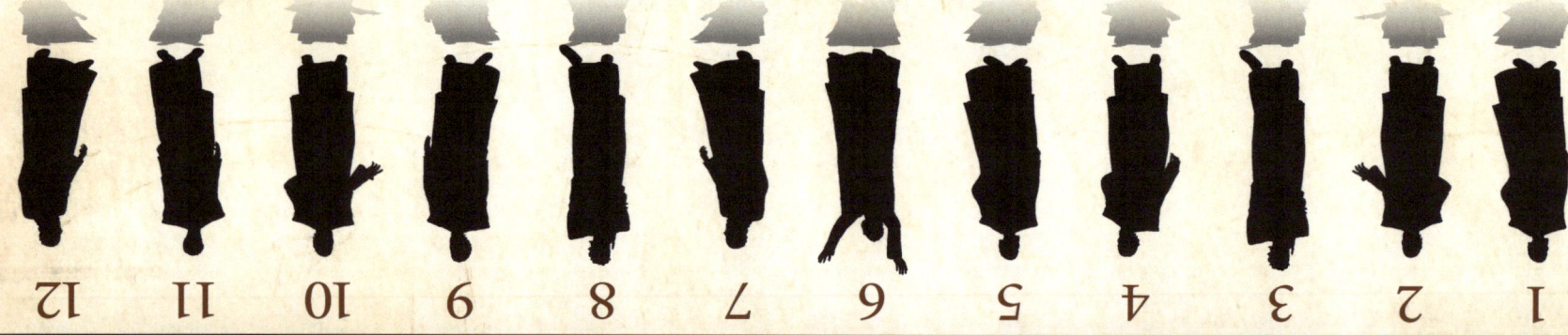

1 2 3 4 5 6 7 8 9 10 11 12

- The 12 were sent to proclaim the gospel of the Kingdom, a message of repentance - Acts 2:38-40
- The 12 were under the leadership of Peter - Matthew 16:19
- The 12 would have 12 thrones, judging Israel - Matt 19:28
- The 12 were to preach Christ as the Messiah, coming to judge Israel and rule over the nations - Acts 3:19-21
- The 12 were sent to teach obedience to the Law for Israel - Matthew 28:19-20, Acts 21:19-20

PAUL

- Paul's salvation and training was outside of all influence of the 12 - Galatians 1:11-12
- Paul was the recipient of a mystery revelation, not a prophetic revelation - Ephesians 3:2-3
- Paul magnified his ministry over that of the 12 - Romans 11:13
- Paul gave no deference to the 12 – Galatians 2:6

Description

A person's doctrine of the apostles will greatly affect their practical Christianity. For example, if you believe that there are modern apostles, that will express itself in modern dreams, visions, miracles, speaking in tongues, and other charismatic expressions. Furthermore, if you do not see a distinction between the role of the 12 apostles in Israel and that of Paul to the Gentiles, you will have an expression of faith that is "Lordship Salvation" rather than "Free Grace" salvation.

Notes

THE PROPHETIC PLAN REVEALED

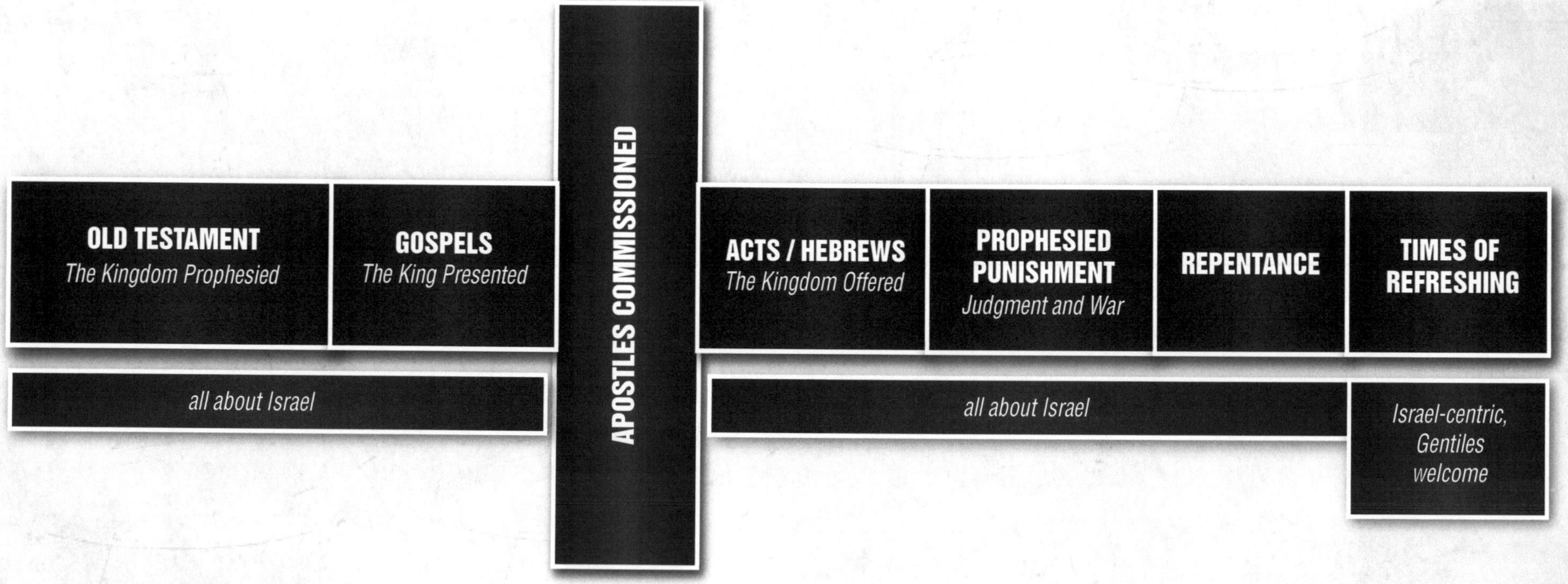

The BIBLE *Graphically Presented*

98

		APOSTLES COMMISSIONED				
OLD TESTAMENT *The Kingdom Prophesied*	GOSPELS *The King Presented*		ACTS / HEBREWS *The Kingdom Offered*	PROPHESIED PUNISHMENT *Judgment and War*	REPENTANCE	TIMES OF REFRESHING

all about Israel | all about Israel | Israel-centric, Gentiles welcome

Description

The Hebrew Scriptures revealed a plan of restoration that included judgment and war on the Hebrew nation when they refused to accept their coming Messiah. That judgment was known as "the Day of the Lord," and would be followed by a repentance of the Jewish people and an acceptance of the Stone that the builders rejected. Repentance would be met by times of refreshing, which was the promised rest the nation has been looking for since the days of the exile. The revealed plan did not include an age of grace that concluded with a rapture, thus the things associated with this current dispensation were described as a mystery.

Notes

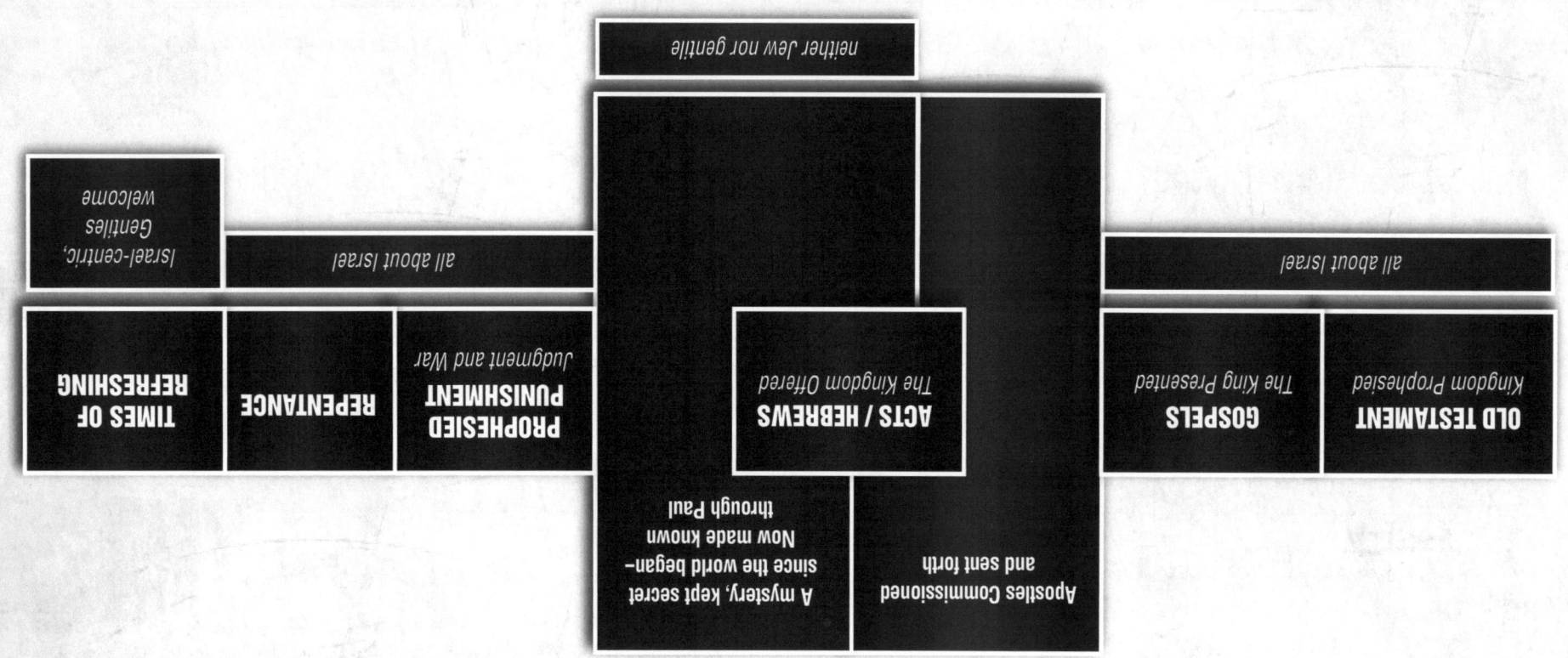

Description

Rather than move immediately into the prophetic program of judgment and war, God initiated an unforeseen age of grace in which he allows "whosoever will" to come unto him, by grace through faith. This unforeseen age will end with a rapture, something that was kept hidden in previous dispensations because it was related to that which was still a mystery. The dispensation of grace is sometimes called the "Mystery Age."

Notes

CHRIST IN THE SCRIPTURES

CHRIST

- **OLD TESTAMENT** → Christ Preincarnate
- **GOSPELS** → Christ in His Earthly Walk
- **ACTS AND THE EPISTLES** → Christ in His Heavenly Realm
- **REVELATION** → Christ in His Future Reign

The **BIBLE** *Graphically Presented*

Description

Jesus Christ is in the Scriptures from beginning to end. He is the Creator, the focus of the law and the prophets, the fulfillment of the theocracy and the monarchy, the suffering servant and the risen King. Today we only know him in the heavenly realm, but in the future the world will know him as King of kings and Lord of lords.

Notes

FREEDOM IN CHRIST

The BIBLE *Graphically Presented*

"let no man therefore judge you." Col 2:16

"Having forgiven you of all your trespasses."
Col. 2:13

"Blotting out the hand-writing of ordinances that was against us."
Col. 2:14

"Having spoiled principalities and powers."
Col. 2:15

Description

In Christ we are complete! When we accept the gift of salvation that is given by grace through faith, a gift that is completely paid for by the work of Jesus Christ, he makes us completely whole, completely forgiven, and completely righteous in Him. Neither our salvation nor sanctification is dependent upon our work. Rather, we glory in Him and celebrate His completed work on the cross. To honor Him for this work, we live lives that honor Him. "…whatsoever ye do, do all to the glory of God" (1 Corinthians 10:31).

Notes

Theology

Chronological Timelines of the Old Testament

INTRODUCTION TO THE TIMELINES

The dates on all of the timelines are anno mundi (AM). This is the number of years since creation and is roughly the number used in the Hebrew calendar. Converting these dates to the Gregorian calendar is challenging and should be done with caution. The following calendars have very few Gregorian dates, and the dates included are well-established in history (such as the fall of Jerusalem in 586 BC).

The study of chronology can be of great assistance to the student of the Bible. As you study, you may want to add notes of Biblical passages to create your own personalized timeline.

The creation of exact timelines is difficult. The periods of the judges and the kings are especially daunting. As you study, you will encounter various chronologies that may differ slightly. The student is encouraged to question the assumptions on all Biblical chronologies, knowing that they are simply the efforts of the study done by another student of the Word.

A BIBLICAL TIMELINE
Adam to Noah

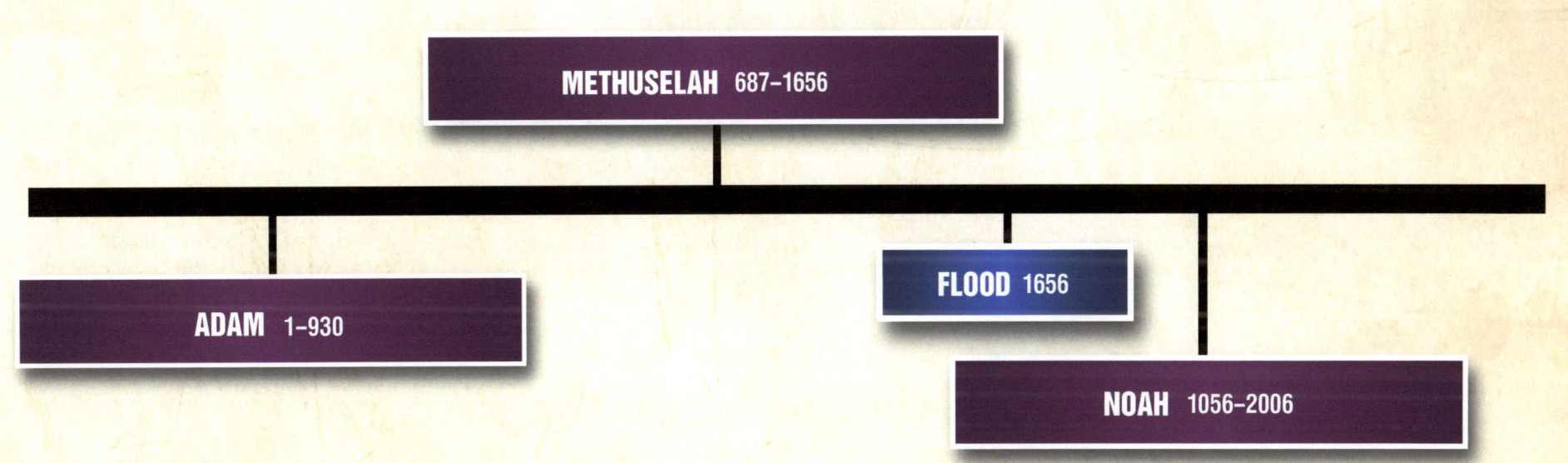

A BIBLICAL TIMELINE
Noah to Abraham

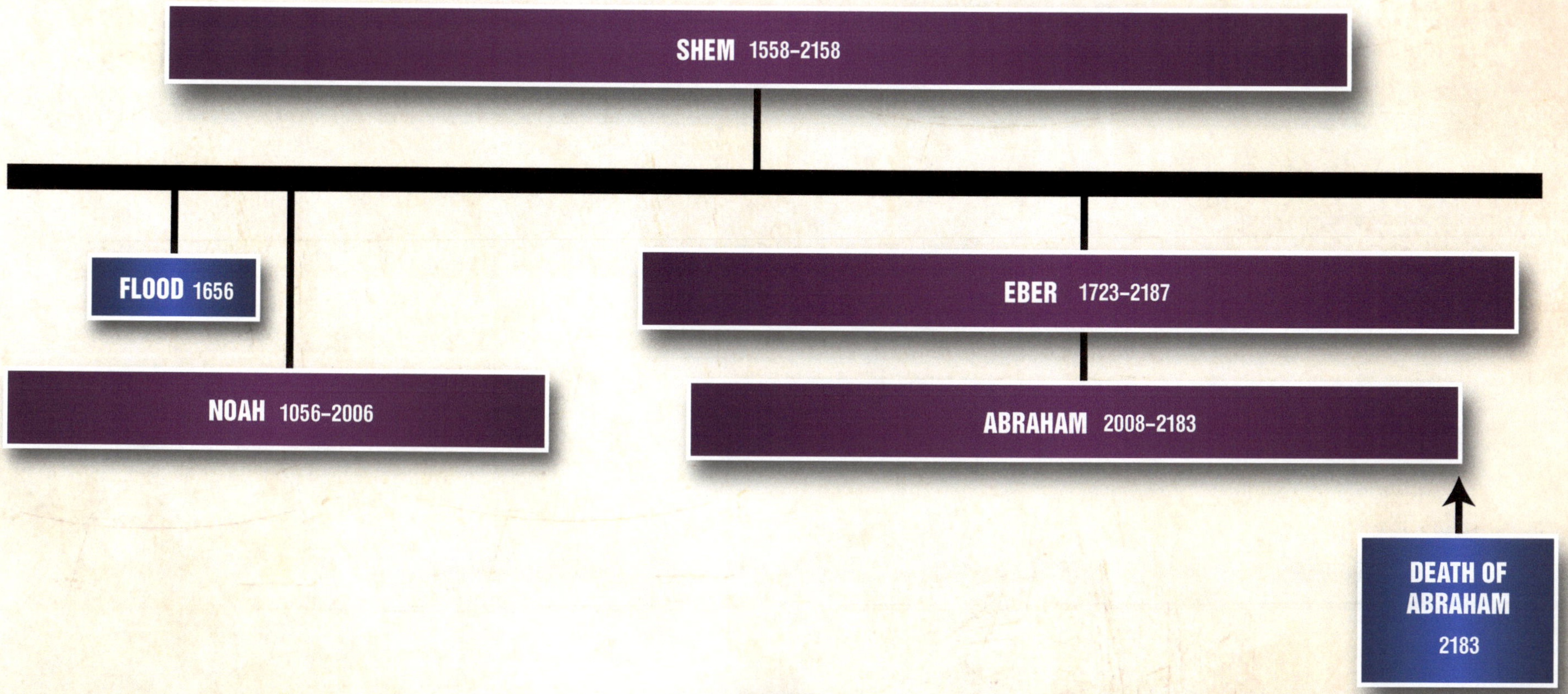

The BIBLE *Graphically Presented*

DEATH OF ABRAHAM 2183

ABRAHAM 2008–2183

EBER 1723–2187

SHEM 1558–2158

NOAH 1056–2006

FLOOD 1656

A BIBLICAL TIMELINE
Abraham to Exodus

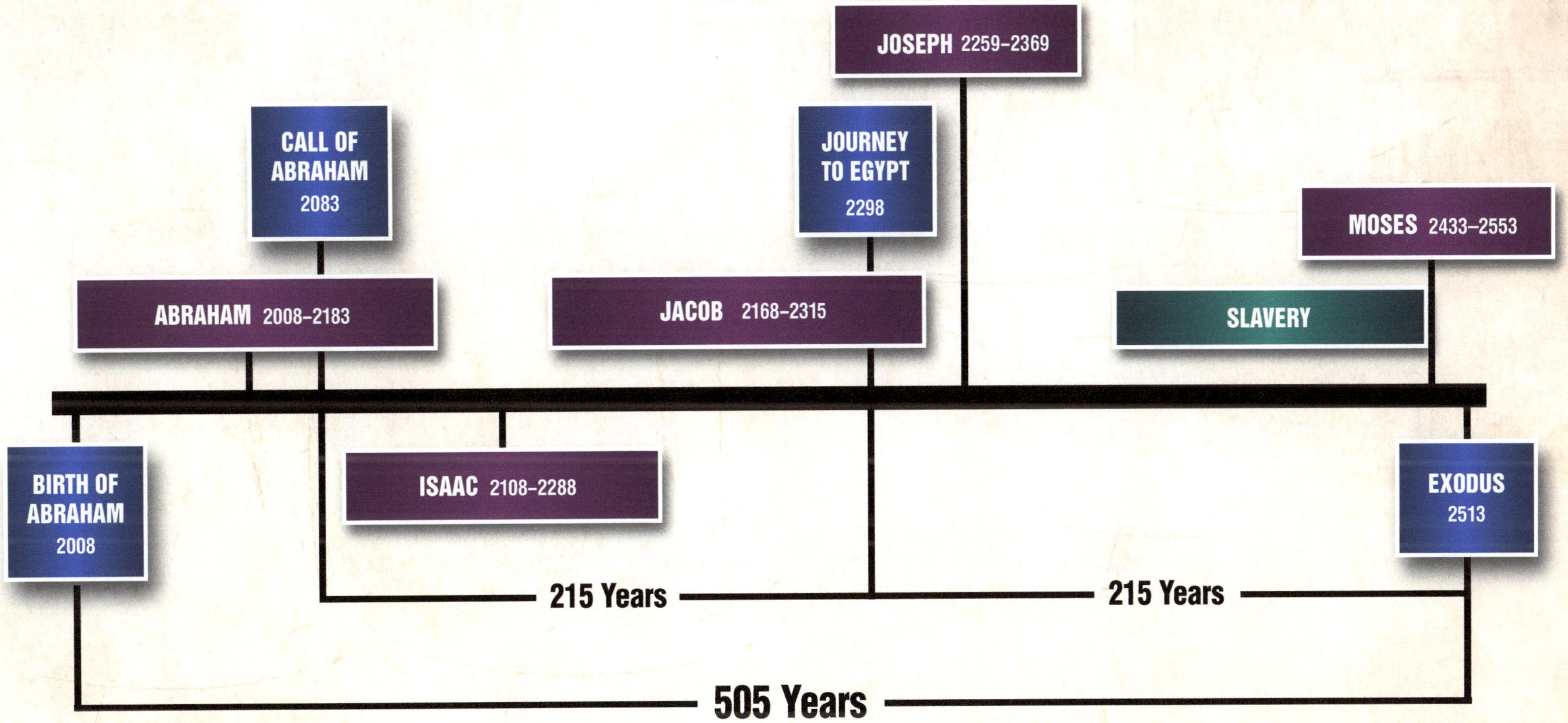

- JOSEPH 2259–2369
- CALL OF ABRAHAM 2083
- JOURNEY TO EGYPT 2298
- MOSES 2433–2553
- ABRAHAM 2008–2183
- JACOB 2168–2315
- SLAVERY
- BIRTH OF ABRAHAM 2008
- ISAAC 2108–2288
- EXODUS 2513

215 Years — 215 Years

505 Years

A BIBLICAL TIMELINE
Exodus to Monarchy

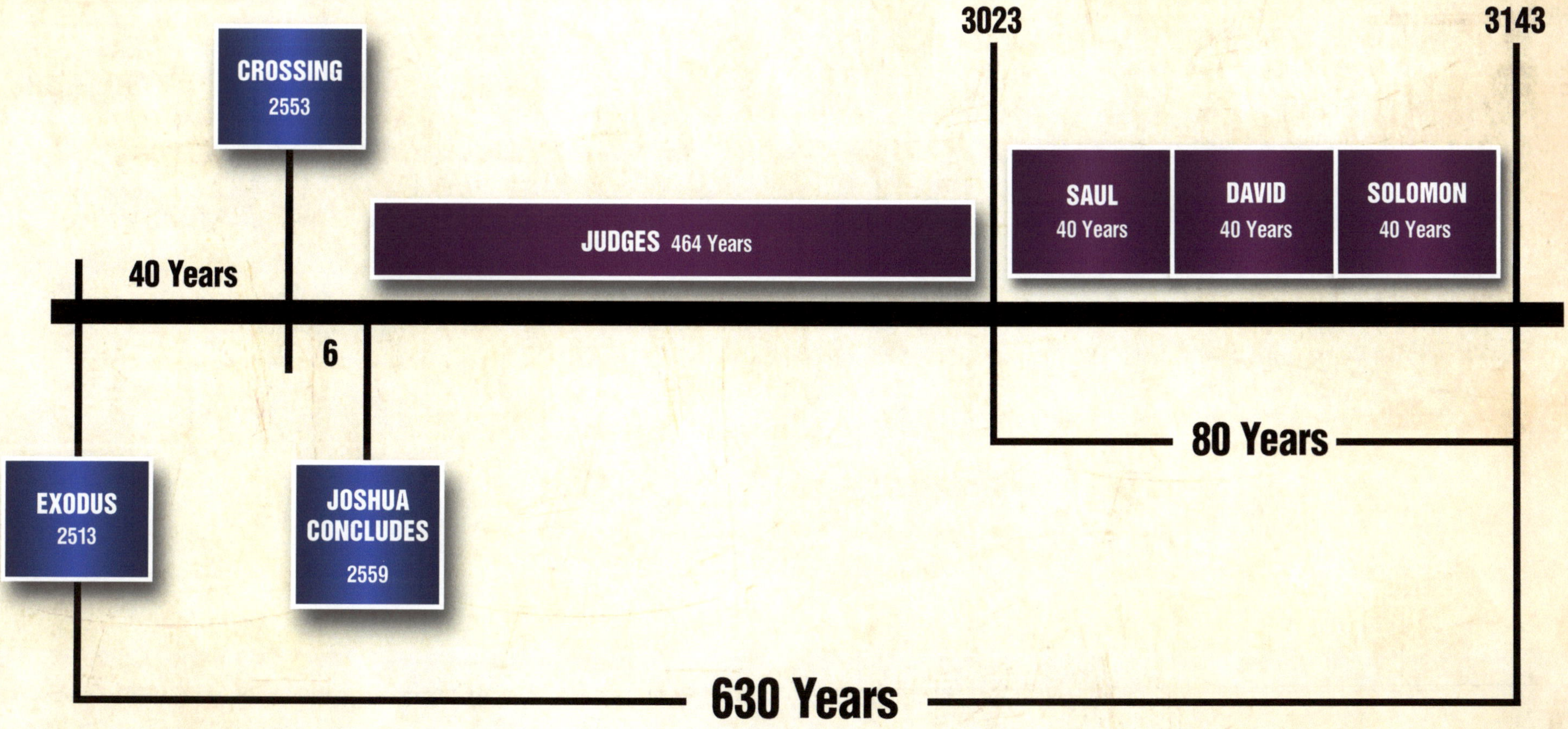

The BIBLE Graphically Presented

630 Years

80 Years

40 Years

- EXODUS 2513
- CROSSING 2553
- JOSHUA CONCLUDES 2559
- JUDGES 464 Years
- SAUL 40 Years
- DAVID 40 Years
- SOLOMON 40 Years

3023

3143

100

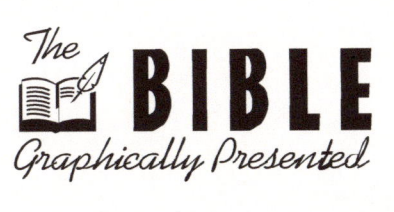

A BIBLICAL TIMELINE
Divided Kingdom

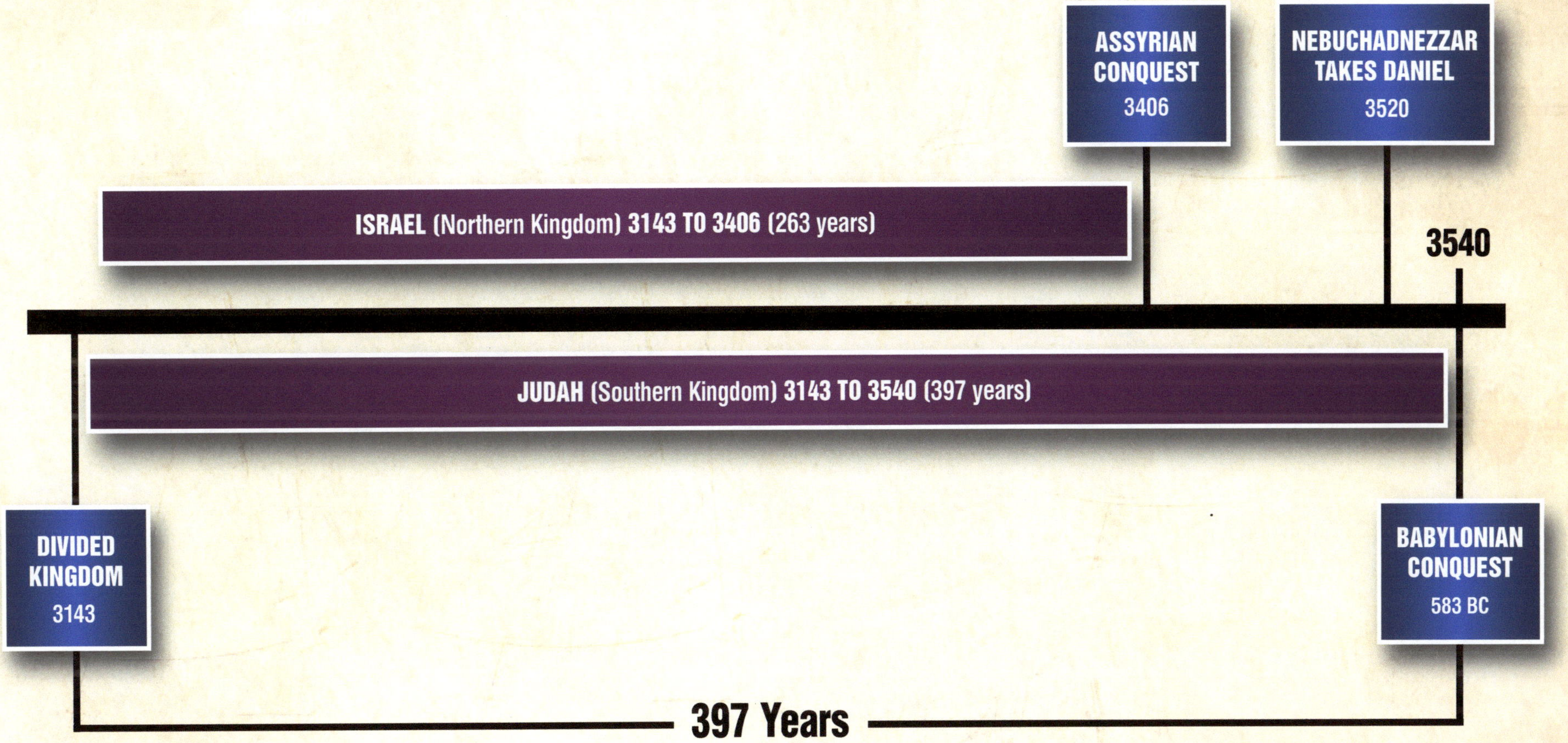

ASSYRIAN CONQUEST 3406

NEBUCHADNEZZAR TAKES DANIEL 3520

ISRAEL (Northern Kingdom) 3143 TO 3406 (263 years)

3540

JUDAH (Southern Kingdom) 3143 TO 3540 (397 years)

DIVIDED KINGDOM 3143

BABYLONIAN CONQUEST 583 BC

397 Years

Dispensational Publishing House is striving to become the go-to source for Bible-based materials from the dispensational perspective.

Our goal is to provide high-quality doctrinal and worldview resources that make dispensational theology accessible to people at all levels of understanding.

Visit our blog regularly to read informative articles from both known and new writers.

And please let us know how we can better serve you.

Dispensational Publishing House, Inc.

Taos, NM 87571

DispensationalPublishing.com